The Very Best of Vivienne Westwood

FRANK JOHNSON

Copyright © 2014 Frank Johnson

All rights reserved.

ISBN: 1502903660
ISBN-13: 978-1502903662

CONTENTS

Introduction	1
About Fashion	3
About Her Work	9
About Herself	17
About Mankind	27
About Other People	31
About Women & Feminism	33
General Thoughts & Opinions	35
On Climate Change	41
Politics & Social Issues	43

INTRODUCTION

Vivienne Westwood is, of course, best known as one of the most renowned names in fashion design. Her works in fashion have revolutionised the industry's landscape and inspired many new trends.

Yet there is much more to Westwood than her extensive work in fashion. She is a symbol of boldness and is well known for her strong and outspoken opinions on a number of subjects.

Though not involved in politics directly, Westwood has been very vocal on many societal issues including climate change, nuclear disarmament and civil liberties. She is also a shrewd businesswoman.

This book brings together some of her most notable quotes on a variety of topics.

ABOUT FASHION

"I think it is a good thing to buy less and choose well - it's good for the environment and to be fair it's also good for me because my clothes are quite expensive."

*

"It's true the punk fashion itself was iconographic: rips and dirt, safety pins, zips, slogans, and hairstyles. These motifs were so iconic in themselves - motifs of rebellion."

*

"I just think people should invest in the world. Don't invest in fashion, but invest in the world."

*

"At one time, I was very angry. I even treated fashion like a kind of crusade: you were either with us or against us, that kind of feeling. Now I know we need ideas, not kicking down a door."

*

"If you wear clothes that don't suit you, you're a fashion victim. You have to wear clothes that make you look better."

*

"If you're too big to fit into fashion, then you just have to do your own fashion."

*

"I don't care if you get up in the morning and don't wash, don't put any make-up on, don't do your hair, even, but you have to have clothes if you want to look different."

*

"I don't think punk fashion is a specter or overemphasized - it made a big impression, as there had never been anything like it before."

*

"I wish you didn't have to design so often. Try to do quality and cut down on quantity. I think fashion is very, very important."

*

"Fashion has become so whatever. I don't think there are any stones left to unturn."

*

"I never look at fashion magazines. I find them incredibly boring."

*

"In history people dressed much better than we do today."

*

"Britishness is just a way of putting things together and a certain don't care attitude about clothes. You don't care, you just do it and it looks great."

*

"Fashion is here to help make people look very important. If they have good taste and choose what suits them, I give them options on how they can do that. It's always sexy, and it's always with the same result: making women look fantastic."

*

"You have a more interesting life if you wear impressive clothes."

*

"My son has followed fashion since he was a punk. He and I agree that fashion is about sex."

*

"Everybody looks like clones and the only people you notice are my age. I don't notice anybody unless they look great, and every now and again they do, and they are usually 70."

*

"Don't just eat McDonald's, get something a bit better. Eat a salad. That's what fashion is. It's something that is a bit better."

*

"Fashion is very important. It is life-enhancing and, like everything that gives pleasure, it is worth doing well."

*

"But, having a perfume and license, in general, is a financial necessity. A designer must, to reap back the money spent on prototypes and all that sort of thing."

*

"I don't care how many beauty treatments you have, I don't care which bag you're carrying - you have to have a dress."

*

"I think dress, hairstyle and make-up are the crucial factors in projecting an attractive persona and give one the chance to enhance one's best physical features."

*

"I'm not sure what I think about current fashion, though. A few years ago, I would have said it's really, really bad and you hardly ever see anybody looking good. There must be some very good designers in the world."

ABOUT HER WORK

"When we started to do punk, we put all of these things together to create the look of an urban guerrilla - a rebel."

*

"However, because Britain is young and exciting, I did show my second line here once or twice."

*

"I have certain signatures, certain cutting principles. It could be a raw-edged seam; it could be leaving the lining of sheepskin exposed so it's not perfectly finished. I invent new ways to do it, but the end goal is always the same."

*

"My clothes are very popular in Japan."

*

"In Italy they take cheap cloth and make it look expensive, but I take expensive cloth and make it look cheap. They just don't understand."

*

"What I'm always trying to say to the consumer is: buy less, choose well, make it last."

*

"I very rarely watch my own fashion shows, but the makeup for my Fall 2011 show was just brilliant."

*

"I have too much product, and I'm trying to rein it in and sell more of my main collection. I wish you didn't have to design so often; it would be good if you could keep on selling the same things for a few years and not have to do new things all the time."

*

"I am always trying to find fabrics that are more friendly to the environment - working with Virgin Atlantic, they managed to research into this and find more eco fabrics."

*

"I have a company, and I've got to think about that. I'm trying to do my best there, and that's a much harder task. We recycle as much as possible, and we conserve. But I've always been one to save everything - I even walk up stairs on the very inside or the very outside to not wear out the tread."

*

"The young Japanese, especially, love to wear the latest thing and when they come to London they head for my shops as part of what they want to find in Britain."

*

"Even though it was the 70s, we found old stocks of clothes that had never been worn from the 50s and took them apart. I started to teach myself how to make clothes from that kind of formula."

*

"The thing that makes my clothes really different is that, number one, they are really great designs; they're not tacky; they are very professional; the design is made from lots of decisions."

*

"I tend not to like an awful lot of what is going out under my name now because it is just all product. Who needs it?"

*

"I love designing at the moment, I'm so happy with my work."

*

"We based the look on rock 'n roll right from the beginning."

*

"I've always had my own access to the public, because I started off making my clothes for a little shop, and so I've always had people buying them. I could always sell a few, even if I couldn't sell a lot, and somehow my business grew because people happened to like it. I'm in a fortunate position."

*

"I've got a real sense of three-dimensional geometry. I can look at a flat piece of fabric and know that if I put a slit in it and make some fabric travel around a square, then when you lift it up it will drape in a certain way, and I can feel how that will happen."

*

"I don't feel comfortable defending my clothes. But if you've got the money to afford them, then buy something from me. Just don't buy too much."

*

"It is extremely difficult to say how long the process actually took to finally achieve my fragrance, Boudoir, because there was a lot of time waiting around for other people."

*

"I don't feel very comfortable defending my fashion except to say that people don't have to buy it. You do have to consume. You have to live. If you've got the money to be able to afford it, then it's really good to buy something from me, but don't buy too much."

*

"I think some people would love to be able to make the clothes I make - and of course, I do influence them, but they keep simplifying, and minimalism doesn't quite work."

*

"I didn't want to be a fashion designer, and for a good half of my career I didn't like it. I always wanted to do other things."

*

"But, the thing is, since I always had my own little shop and direct access to the public, I've been able to build up a technique without marketing people ever telling me what the public wants."

*

"I'm different from any other designer, businesswise, in that I've built this company up and I own it. I never had business hype behind me to promote my image... My image is real... I have never had marketing people telling me what to do."

*

"My clothes have always got a very strong dynamic rapport with the body - they are very body conscious, they help you to look glamorous, more hourglass, more woman."

*

"I design things to help people to hopefully express their personality."

*

"I'm a fashion designer and people think, what do I know?"

*

"My aim is to make the poor look rich and the rich look poor."

ABOUT HERSELF

"The hippie movement politicized my generation. When it ended, we all started looking back at our own history, looking, in my case, for motives of rebellion."

*

"When I first saw a picture of the crucifixion, I lost respect for my parents. I suddenly realised that this is what the adult world is like - full of cruelty and hypocrisy."

*

"Personally I'm not a feminist, as I can't stand puritans."

*

"I eat only vegetables and fruit, and to me it's the most aspirational diet because it's so easy. It's quite simple, the cooking I do."

*

"I think I've got wiser."

*

"I always tried to do things by example, even though I was not a very good mother regarding routines and family life."

*

"What I remember as a child is that other kids didn't care about suffering. I always did."

*

"What changed our lives forever was when Malcolm had the idea to sell rock 'n roll records to trendy customers."

*

"My children came out as individuals in their own right. They were not my products. They had their own characters and were very strong-minded. I gave them a lot of freedom when they were still very young. The one thing they got from me is morals. They would never betray anyone. They are really good people."

*

"I've always felt heroic about my life... As a child, I remember little girls in the playground moaning about how boys could do more than they could. I didn't think that was the case at all. My parents didn't treat me as a girl."

*

"I've got a terrible memory; it's probably because I'm always concentrating on what I'm doing now."

*

"I don't watch television and I rarely go to the cinema, but I recently watched 'The King's Speech' on a flight. It was so beautiful and so simple."

*

"I don't have faith in young people anymore. I don't waste time trying to communicate with them."

*

"In the morning, I practice 15 minutes of yoga."

*

"I disagree with everything I used to say."

*

"I can't think without my glasses."

*

"I am in my own head most of the time."

*

"I was born during the war and grew up in a time of rationing. We didn't have anything. It's influenced the way I look at the world."

*

"Every time I have to look up a word in the dictionary, I'm delighted."

*

"When I was a little girl you used to learn to sew all the holes in things, darning socks, but nobody mends things anymore."

*

"I am attracted to people who make this effort in knowing what suits them - they are individual and stylish."

*

"I'm very lucky. The public happens to like me. Maybe they like me because I use every opportunity to talk about injustice."

*

"My beauty secret is absolutely no sun."

*

"I'd like to be the last person alive in the world! Yes, I'd like to know what happens."

*

"I'm frugal. I'm not a very acquisitive woman. I never waste food. If you prepare your own food, you engage with the world, it tastes alive. It tastes good."

*

"The best night of my life was watching the Japanese Noh theater. I've only seen it once, but even saying it now, I think, 'How can I ever have this experience again?' It was so mesmerizing, so complicated and so primordial; I could not believe it."

*

"I'll tell you what I was like as a child. I was a good person. I was high-spirited but I was a big reader."

*

"I have been asked what would I ban immediately if I could. Advertising."

*

"I was the first person to have a punk rock hairstyle."

*

"I was still interested in the youth rebellion but nevertheless I stopped being a victim. Stopped trying to attack the establishment realizing that it takes too much of your energy."

*

"I was a punk before it got its name. I had that hairstyle and purple lipstick."

*

"To me, reading a fashion magazine is the last thing I need to do. I've got books I need to read."

*

"I didn't consider myself a fashion designer at all at the time of punk. I was just using fashion as a way to express my resistance and to be rebellious. I came from the country, and by the time I got to London, I considered myself to be very stupid. It was my ambition to understand the world I live in."

*

"We moved into the back, made it into a little 50s sitting room and started to sell the records. We had an immediate success. For one thing, these Teddy Boys were thrilled to buy the records."

*

"Home, more than anything, means warmth and bed."

ABOUT MANKIND

"The muscular, athletic type is not representative of the human race, who are varied in their physique."

*

"You've got to invest in the world, you've got to read, you've got to go to art galleries, you've got to find out the names of plants. You've got to start to love the world and know about the whole genius of the human race. We're amazing people."

*

"People have never looked so ugly as they do today. We just consume far too much."

*

"There is no hierarchy of values any more. Real progress is due mainly to human genius, and that's rare, and usually stems from a real elite, from a hierarchy."

*

"The last people with any ideas are young people."

*

"It is not possible for a man to be elegant without a touch of femininity."

*

"We are the most amazing creatures that this world has ever produced, but we seem to also have this herd mentality; we seem to be the most stupid, also."

*

"All that self-expression has just created a generation of morons, hooked on an endless appetite for rubbish."

*

"I do think we're an endangered species. But that we do have a plan to save the rainforest."

ABOUT OTHER PEOPLE

"I didn't do anything at the Queen, whom I admire."

*

"The bravery shown by Azza Suleiman who dared to stand up for another woman who was being beaten, and paid a heavy price in doing so, is both awe-inspiring and humbling."

*

"I always thought we had an environmental problem, but I hadn't realized how urgent it was. James Lovelock writes that by the end of this century there will be one billion people left."

*

"I urge everyone to be trendsetters for Azza Suleiman. Let's make it one fashion which everyone will want to follow."

*

"I'm always attracted to people who interest me. They've got to be people who are really true to themselves somehow, and who are always trying to do something that makes their life more interesting, or better, or something for somebody else. They're interested in people."

*

"If you saw Queen Elizabeth it would be amazing, she came from another planet. She was so attractive in what she was wearing."

*

"Prince Charles is definitely my hero; he uses his position to do only good in this world."

ABOUT WOMEN & FEMINISM

"I think feminists are unaware of the tremendous extent of the role of women in history."

*

"If you see everything from the point of view of women being victims in some way, you don't see the wood for the trees. It is better to be a person than a woman."

*

"I really don't like women who try to be men. All these politicians, I think they're horrendous. We could have a brilliant future, but we have this terrible male vision of destroying everything. They'd better sort themselves out and become more womanly."

*

"Feminists wish women to seem like men. They're not men."

GENERAL THOUGHTS & OPINIONS

"Buy less. Choose well. Make it last. Quality, not quantity. Everybody's buying far too many clothes."

*

"My biggest criticism is how can people be so easily satisfied? Even people with talent."

*

"It's a philosophy of life. A practice. If you do this, something will change, what will change is that you will change, your life will change, and if you can change you, you can perhaps change the world."

*

"Being part of a community with a church at its centre and singin' hymns is a great thing to do."

*

"Real art has been... what's the word? Kidnapped? No, that's not it. But, OK, kidnapped by business."

*

"The arts have only ever interested a small minority of people, which acted as a kind of nursery to support artists."

*

"If we didn't have the Chinese buying things, we'd be on the floor."

*

"There is so much that people take for granted."

*

"More people should read books. It's the most concentrated experience you can have."

*

"Popular culture is a contradiction in terms. If it's popular, it's not culture."

*

"Liverpool people are famous for liking clothes and fashion; they are very social and lively people, and we know that they like clothes."

*

"I don't have space to enter into the examples or the history of this, so I'm left with having to make the bold statement that culture is extinct."

*

"There's nowhere else like London. Nothing at all, anywhere."

*

"The sexiest people are thinkers. Nobody's interested in somebody who's just vain with a hole in their head, talking about the latest thing - there is no latest thing. It's all rubbish."

*

"Instead of buying six things, buy one thing that you really like. Don't keep buying just for the sake of it."

*

"The only possible effect one can have on the world is through unpopular ideas."

*

"The French have got taste."

*

"I'm the proof - you can't throw away tradition."

*

"I do not approve of museums trying just to get people to come in. Whistler was very, very clear on this."

ON CLIMATE CHANGE

"Print some money and give it to us for the rain forests."

*

"The main message we want to get out there is that climate change is caused by the rotten economic system."

*

"I talk to fashion designers and say I want some money to save the rainforest, and they say, 'Oh, I agree with you completely Vivienne. Yes, climate change, it's definitely happening,' but they don't feel that they can do anything about it; they don't even think 'Well let's stop it!'"

*

"Our economic system, run for profit and waste and based primarily on the extractive industries, is the cause of climate change. We have wasted the earth's treasure and we can no longer exploit it cheaply."

*

"The main message of Climate Revolution is that climate change is caused by the rotten financial system we've got, designed to create poverty and rip off any profits for a small amount of rich people. Meanwhile, it destroys the earth."

POLITICS & SOCIAL ISSUES

"The age in which we live, this non-stop distraction, is making it more impossible for the young generation to ever have the curiosity or discipline... because you need to be alone to find out anything."

*

"I don't follow politics much."

*

"I think that feminists have definitely underestimated the role that women have had historically. I think I would be insecure if I were to be a man; there's so much pressure on you."

*

"We have got to change our ethics and our financial system and our whole way of understanding the world. It has to be a world in which people live rather than die; a sustainable world. It could be great."

*

"I used to always fight for human rights. I still fight for Leonard Peltier, who's spent 35 years in jail for a crime he didn't commit."

*

"We are so conformist; nobody is thinking. We are all sucking up stuff; we have been trained to be consumers, and we are all consuming far too much."

*

"The reason why I am proud of my part in the punk movement is that I think it really did implant a message that was already there. The hippies told it to me, but punk made it something cool for people to stand up for, which is that we do not believe government, that we are against government."

*

"Women fight for democracy and engage in the world. But they shouldn't try and be copying men and be masculine; they should anchor on the home and build on those fundamentals."

*

"I think it's important to vote."

*

"Everybody should have a fair deal; everybody should have the chance to life in this world. If we were evolved as human beings, we would hopefully be able to alleviate suffering in the world."

*

"If you hear Anarchy in the UK today your hair stands on end. It gives you the shivers."

*

"The capitalist system is about taking from the Earth and from the other great commodity, labour. What's happening with this system is that the rich are getting richer and the poor are getting poorer, and the only way out of it is supposed to be growth. But growth is debt. It's going to make the situation worse."

*

"I was so upset with what was going on in the world. I just couldn't stand the idea of being people tortured and that we even had such a thing as war. I hated the older generation, who had not done anything about it. Punk was a call-to-arms for me."

*

"I have considered voting Conservative because I am so against the Labour party."

*

"I just use fashion as an excuse to talk about politics. Because I'm a fashion designer, it gives me a voice, which is really good."

*

"Economists treat economics as if it is a pure science divorced from the facts of life. The result of this false accountancy is a willful confusion under cover of which industry wreaks its havoc scot-free and ignores the environmental cost."

ALSO BY FRANK JOHNSON

INSIDE THE MIND OF CHUCK PALAHNIUK

THE WIT AND WISDOM OF JOSS WHEDON

INSIDE THE MIND OF EMMA WATSON

THE VERY BEST OF MICHAEL MOORE

THE PHILOSOPHY OF PAUL WATSON

Printed in Great Britain
by Amazon